Published in Great Britain by Brimax Publishing Ltd
Appledram Barns, Chichester PO20 7EQ
© Brimax Publishing Ltd 2005

Printed in China

My Little
Rhyme and
Verse
Treasury

Humpty Dumpty

Humpty Dumpty sat on a wall,
Humpty Dumpty had a great fall.
All the king's horses and all the king's men,
Couldn't put Humpty together again.

Old King Cole

Old King Cole
Was a merry old soul,
And a merry old soul was he;
He called for his pipe,
And he called for his bowl,
And he called for his fiddlers three.

There was a Crooked Man

There was a crooked man, and he walked a crooked mile,
He found a crooked sixpence against a crooked stile;
He bought a crooked cat, which caught a crooked mouse,
And they all lived together in a little crooked house.

Wee Willie Winkie

Wee Willie Winkie runs through the town,
Upstairs and downstairs in his nightgown.
Rapping at the window, crying through the lock,
'Are the children all in bed, for now it's eight o'clock?'

A Cat Came Fiddling

A cat came fiddling out of a barn,
With a pair of bagpipes under her arm,
She could sing nothing but fiddle cum fee,
The mouse has married the bumble-bee.
Pipe, cat; dance, mouse;
We'll have a wedding at our good house.

Little Miss Muffet

Little Miss Muffet
Sat on a tuffet,
Eating her curds and whey;
There came a big spider,
Who sat down beside her
And frightened Miss Muffet away.

What Are Little Boys Made Of?

What are little boys made of?
What are little boys made of?
Frogs and snails
And puppy-dogs' tails,
That's what little boys are made of.

What are little girls made of?
What are little girls made of?
Sugar and spice
And all things nice,
That's what little girls are made of.

Hickety, Pickety,
My Black Hen

Hickety, pickety, my black hen,
She lays eggs for gentlemen;
Gentlemen come every day
To see what my black hen doth lay.
Sometimes nine and sometimes ten,
Hickety, pickety, my black hen.

Doctor Foster

Doctor Foster went to Gloucester
In a shower of rain;
He stepped in a puddle,
Right up to his middle,
And never went there again.

Three Blind Mice

Three blind mice, see how they run!
They all ran after the farmer's wife,
Who cut off their tails with a carving knife,
Did you ever see such a thing in your life,
As three blind mice?

There Was an Old Woman

There was an old woman
Lived under a hill,
And if she's not gone
She lives there still.

The North Wind

The North wind doth blow,
And we shall have snow,
And what will poor robin do then?
Poor thing.
He'll sit in a barn,
And keep himself warm,
And hide his head under his wing.
Poor thing.

Mary had a Little Lamb

Mary had a little lamb,
Its fleece was white as snow;
And everywhere that Mary went
The lamb was sure to go.

It followed her to school one day,
That was against the rule;
It made the children laugh and play
To see a lamb at school.

And so the teacher turned it out,
But still it lingered near,
And waited patiently about
Till Mary did appear.

'Why does the lamb love Mary so?'
The eager children cry;
'Why, Mary loves the lamb, you know,'
The teacher did reply.

There was a Little Girl

There was a little girl, and she had a little curl
Right in the middle of her forehead;
And when she was good, she was very, very good,
And when she was bad, she was horrid.

Peter Piper

Peter Piper picked a peck of pickled pepper;
A peck of pickled pepper Peter Piper picked;
If Peter Piper picked a peck of pickled pepper,
Where's the peck of pickled pepper Peter Piper picked?

Hush-a-bye, Baby

Hush-a-bye, baby, on the tree top,
When the wind blows the cradle will rock;
When the bough breaks the cradle will fall,
Down will come baby, cradle, and all.

Up in a Basket

There was an old woman tossed up in a basket,
Seventeen times as high as the moon;
Where she was going I couldn't but ask it,
For in her hand she carried a broom.
'Old woman, old woman, old woman,' quoth I,
'Where are you going to up so high?'
'To brush the cobwebs off the sky!'
'May I go with you?'
'Aye, by and by.'

Little Jack Horner

Little Jack Horner
Sat in a corner,
Eating a Christmas pie;
He put in his thumb,
And pulled out a plum,
And said, 'What a good boy am I!'

Handy Spandy, Jack-a-Dandy

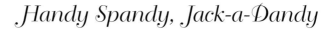

Handy Spandy, Jack-a-Dandy,
Loves plum cake and sugar candy;
He bought some at a grocer's shop,
And out he came, hop, hop, hop.

A Wise Old Owl

A wise old owl lived in an oak;
The more he saw the less he spoke;
The less he spoke the more he heard.
Why can't we all be like that wise old bird?

Three Ships

I saw three ships come sailing by,
Come sailing by, come sailing by,
I saw three ships come sailing by,
On New Year's Day in the morning.

And what do you think was in them then,
Was in them then, was in them then?
And what do you think was in them then,
On New Year's Day in the morning?

Three pretty girls were in them then,
Were in them then, were in them then,
Three pretty girls were in them then,
On New Year's Day in the morning.

One could whistle, and one could sing,
And one could play on the violin;
Such joy there was at my wedding,
On New Year's Day in the morning.

Ride a Cock-horse

Ride a cock-horse to Banbury Cross,
To see a fine lady upon a white horse;
Rings on her fingers and bells on her toes,
And she shall have music wherever she goes.

If All the World were Paper

If all the world were paper,
And all the sea were ink,
If all the trees were bread and cheese,
What should we have to drink?

There was an Old Woman

There was an old woman who lived in a shoe,
She had so many children she didn't know what to do;
She gave them some broth without any bread;
She whipped them all soundly and put them to bed.

The Moon

I see the moon,
And the moon sees me;
God bless the moon,
And God bless me.

The Queen of Hearts

The Queen of Hearts
She made some tarts,
All on a summer's day;
The Knave of Hearts
He stole the tarts,
And took them clean away.

The King of Hearts
Called for the tarts,
And beat the Knave full sore;
The Knave of Hearts
Brought back the tarts,
And vowed he'd steal no more.

The Little Hen

I had a little hen,
The prettiest ever seen;
She washed up the dishes,
And kept the house clean.
She went to the mill
To fetch me some flour,
And always got home
In less than an hour.
She baked me my bread,
She brewed me my ale,
She sat by the fire
And told a fine tale.

Diddle, Diddle, Dumpling

Diddle, diddle, dumpling, my son John,
Went to bed with his trousers on;
One shoe off, and one shoe on,
Diddle, diddle, dumpling, my son John.

Jack Sprat

Jack Sprat could eat no fat,
His wife could eat no lean,
And so between them both, you see,
They licked the platter clean.

Polly Put the Kettle on

Polly put the kettle on,
Polly put the kettle on,
Polly put the kettle on,
We'll all have tea.

Sukey take it off again,
Sukey take it off again,
Sukey take it off again,
They've all gone away.

The Grand Old Duke of York

Oh, the grand old Duke of York,
He had ten thousand men;
He marched them up to the top of the hill,
And he marched them down again.
And when they were up, they were up,
And when they were down, they were down,
And when they were only halfway up,
They were neither up nor down.

Punch and Judy

Punch and Judy
Fought for pie;
Punch gave Judy
A knock in the eye.
Says Punch to Judy,
'Will you have any more?'
Says Judy to Punch,
'My eye is sore.'

Pease Porridge Hot

Pease porridge hot,
Pease porridge cold,
Pease porridge in the pot,
Nine days old.

Some like it hot,
Some like it cold,
Some like it in the pot
Nine days old.

One, Two, Three, Four

One, two, three, four,
Mary at the cottage door,
Five, six, seven, eight,
Eating cherries off a plate.

Peter, Peter, Pumpkin Eater

Peter, Peter, pumpkin eater,
Had a wife and couldn't keep her;
He put her in a pumpkin shell
And there he kept her very well.

Baa, Baa, Black Sheep

Baa, baa, black sheep,
Have you any wool?
Yes, sir, yes, sir,
Three bags full;
One for the master,
And one for the dame,
And one for the little boy
Who lives down the lane.

Goosey, Goosey, Gander

Goosey, goosey, gander,
Whither shall I wander?
Upstairs and downstairs
And in my lady's chamber.
There I met an old man
Who would not say his prayers.
I took him by the left leg
And threw him down the stairs.

There was a Little Boy

There was a little boy went into a barn,
And lay down on some hay;
An owl came out and flew about,
And the little boy ran away.

Mary, Mary, Quite Contrary

Mary, Mary, quite contrary,
How does your garden grow?
With silver bells and cockle shells,
And pretty maids all in a row.

Simple Simon

Simple Simon met a pieman,
Going to the fair;
Says Simple Simon to the pieman,
'Let me taste your ware.'

Says the pieman to Simple Simon,
'Show me first your penny.'
Says Simple Simon to the pieman,
'Indeed I have not any.'

Simple Simon went a-fishing,
For to catch a whale;
All the water he had got
Was in his mother's pail.

Simple Simon went to look
If plums grew on a thistle;
He pricked his fingers very much
Which made poor Simon whistle.

He went for water in a sieve
But soon it all fell through;
And now poor Simple Simon
Bids you all adieu.

If All the Seas were One Sea

If all the seas were one sea,
What a great sea that would be!
If all the trees were one tree,
What a great tree that would be!
If all the axes were one axe,
What a great axe that would be!
And if all the men were one man,
What a great man that would be!
And if the great man took the great axe,
And cut down the great tree,
And let it fall into the great sea,
What a splish-splash that would be!

Jack and Jill

Jack and Jill went up the hill
To fetch a pail of water;
Jack fell down and broke his crown,
And Jill came tumbling after.

Up Jack got, and home did trot,
As fast as he could caper,
He went to bed and patched his head
With vinegar and brown paper.

Rock-a-bye Baby

Rock-a-bye baby,
Thy cradle is green,
Father's a nobleman,
Mother's a queen;
And Betty's a lady,
And wears a gold ring;
And Johnny's a drummer,
And drums for the king.

Hey Diddle Diddle

Hey diddle diddle,
The cat and the fiddle,
The cow jumped over the moon;
The little dog laughed to see such sport,
And the dish ran away with the spoon.

Six Little Mice

Six little mice sat down to spin;
Pussy passed by and she peeped in.
'What are you doing, my little men?'
'Weaving coats for gentlemen.'
'Shall I come in and cut off your threads?'
'No, no, Mistress Pussy, you'd bite off our heads.'
'Oh no, I'll not; I'll help you to spin.'
'That may be so, but you don't come in.'

Ride a Cock-horse

Ride a cock-horse
To Banbury Cross,
To see what Tommy can buy;
A penny white loaf,
A penny white cake,
And a two-penny apple pie.

Twinkle, Twinkle, Little Star

Twinkle, twinkle, little star,
How I wonder what you are!
Up above the world so high,
Like a diamond in the sky.

When the blazing sun is gone,
When he nothing shines upon,
Then you show your little light,
Twinkle, twinkle, all the night.

Then the traveller in the dark
Thanks you for your tiny spark,
He could not see which way to go,
If you did not twinkle so.

In the dark blue sky you keep,
And often through my curtains peep,
For you never shut your eye,
Till the sun is in the sky.

As your bright and tiny spark
Lights the traveller in the dark,
Though I know not what you are,
Twinkle, twinkle, little star.

Oh Where Has My Little Dog Gone?

Oh where, oh where has my little dog gone?
Oh where, oh where can he be?
With his ears cut short and his tail cut long,
Oh where, oh where is he?

Pussy Cat Mole

Pussy Cat Mole jumped over a coal
And in her best petticoat burnt a great hole.
Poor Pussy's weeping, she'll have no more milk
Until her best petticoat's mended with silk.

See-saw, Margery Daw

See-saw, Margery Daw,
Johnny shall have a new master;
Johnny shall have but a penny a day,
Because he can't work any faster.

Little Polly Flinders

Little Polly Flinders
Sat among the cinders,
Warming her pretty little toes;
Her mother came and caught her,
And whipped her little daughter
For spoiling her nice new clothes.

The Old Woman

The old woman must stand at the tub, tub, tub,
The dirty clothes to rub, rub, rub;
But when they are clean, and fit to be seen,
She'll dress like a lady, and dance on the green.

One, Two, Three, Four, Five

One, two, three, four, five,
Once I caught a fish alive,
Six, seven, eight, nine, ten,
Then I let it go again.

Why did you let it go?
Because it bit my finger so.
Which finger did it bite?
This little finger on the right.

Sing a Song of Sixpence

Sing a song of sixpence,
A pocket full of rye;
Four and twenty blackbirds
Baked in a pie.

When the pie was opened,
The birds began to sing;
Was that not a dainty dish
To set before the king?

The king was in his counting house,
Counting out his money;
The queen was in the parlour,
Eating bread and honey.

The maid was in the garden
Hanging out the clothes,
There came a little blackbird,
And snapped off her nose.

This Little Pig went to Market

This little pig went to market,
This little pig stayed at home,
This little pig had roast beef,
This little pig had none,
And this little pig cried,
'Wee-wee-wee-wee-wee,'
All the way home.

Once I Saw a Little Bird

Once I saw a little bird
Come hop, hop, hop,
And I cried, 'Little bird,
Will you stop, stop, stop?'

I was going to the window
To say, 'How do you do?'
But he shook his little tail
And away he flew.

Little Bo-Peep

Little Bo-Peep has lost her sheep,
And can't tell where to find them;
Leave them alone, and they'll come home,
And bring their tails behind them.

Little Bo-Peep fell fast asleep,
And dreamt she heard them bleating;
And when she awoke, she found it a joke,
For they were still all fleeting.

Then up she took her little crook,
Determined for to find them;
She found them indeed, but it made her heart bleed,
For they'd left their tails behind them.

It happened one day, as Bo-Peep did stray
Into a meadow hard by,
There she espied their tails side by side,
All hung on a tree to dry.

She heaved a sigh, and wiped her eye,
And over the hillocks went rambling,
And tried what she could, as a shepherdess should,
To tack again each to its lambkin.

How Many Miles to Babylon?

How many miles to Babylon?
Three score miles and ten.
Can I get there by candle-light?
Yes, and back again.
If your heels are nimble and light,
You may get there by candle-light.

Hot Cross Buns!

Hot cross buns!
Hot cross buns!
One a penny, two a penny,
Hot cross buns!
If your daughters do not like them
Give them to your sons,
But if you haven't any of these, pretty little elves,
You cannot do better than eat them yourselves.

Ladybird, Ladybird

Ladybird, ladybird,
Fly away home,
Your house is on fire
And your children all gone;
All except one
And that's little Ann,
And she has crept under
The warming pan.

Little Boy Blue

Little Boy Blue,
Come blow your horn,
The sheep's in the meadow,
The cow's in the corn.
But where is the boy
Who looks after the sheep?
He's under a haystack,
Fast asleep.
Will you wake him?
No, not I,
For if I do,
He's sure to cry.

As I was Going to St Ives

As I was going to St Ives,
I met a man with seven wives,
Each wife had seven sacks,
Each sack had seven cats,
Each cat had seven kits.
Kits, cats, sacks and wives,
How many were going to St Ives?

Ring-a-ring O' Roses

Ring-a-ring o' roses,
A pocket full of posies,
A-tishoo! A-tishoo!
We all fall down.

Three Little Kittens

Three little kittens they lost their mittens,
And they began to cry,
'Oh, mother dear, we sadly fear
That we have lost our mittens.'
'What! Lost your mittens, you naughty kittens!
Then you shall have no pie.'
'Meow, meow, meow.
No, we shall have no pie.'

The three little kittens they found their mittens,
And they began to cry,
'Oh, mother dear, see here, see here,
For we have found our mittens.'
'Put on your mittens, you silly kittens,
And you shall have some pie.'
'Purr, purr, purr,
Oh, let us have some pie.'

The three little kittens put on their mittens,
And soon ate up the pie.
'Oh, mother dear, we greatly fear
That we have soiled our mittens.'
'What! Soiled your mittens, you naughty kittens!'
Then they began to sigh,
'Meow, meow, meow.'
Then they began to sigh.

The three little kittens they washed their mittens,
And hung them out to dry.
'Oh, mother dear, do you not hear
That we have washed our mittens?'
'What! Washed your mittens, then you're good kittens,
But I smell a rat close by.'
'Meow, meow, meow.
We smell a rat close by.'

Yankee Doodle

Yankee Doodle came to town,
Riding on a pony;
He stuck a feather in his cap
And called it macaroni.

Ding, Dong, Bell

Ding, dong, bell,
Pussy's in the well.
Who put her in?
Little Johnny Green.
Who pulled her out?
Little Tommy Stout.
What a naughty boy was that,
To try to drown poor pussy cat,
Who never did him any harm,
And killed the mice in his father's barn.

Come, Let's to Bed

'Come, let's to bed,'
Says Sleepy-head;
'Tarry awhile,' says Slow;
'Put on the pot,'
Says Greedy-gut,
'We'll sup before we go.'

The Lonely Scarecrow

Mr poor old bones – I've only two
A broomshank and a broken stave,
My ragged gloves are a disgrace
My one peg-foot is in the grave.

I wear the labourer's old clothes;
Coat, shirt and trousers all undone.
I bear my cross upon a hill
In rain and shine, in snow and sun.

I cannot help the way I look.
My funny hat is full of hay.
O, wild birds, come and nest in me!
Why do you always fly away?

James Kirkup

The Eagle

He clasps the crag with crooked hands;
Close to the sun in lonely lands,
Ring'd with the azure world, he stands.

The wrinkled sea beneath him crawls;
He watches from his mountain walls,
And like a thunderbolt he falls.

Alfred, Lord Tennyson

On the Ning Nang Nong

On the Ning Nang Nong
Where the cows go Bong!
And the monkeys all say Boo!
There's a Nong Nang Ning
Where the trees go Ping!
And the teapots Jibber Jabber Joo.
On the Nong Ning Nang
All the mice go Clang!
And you just can't catch 'em when they do!
So it's Ning Nang Nong!
Cows go Bong!
Nong Nang Ning!
Trees go Ping!
Nong Ning Nang!
The mice go Clang!
What a noisy place to belong,
Is the Ning Nang Ning Nang Nong!!

Spike Milligan

Jack Frost

Look out! Look out!
Jack Frost is about!
He's after our fingers and toes;
And all through the night,
The gay little sprite
Is working where nobody knows.

He'll climb each tree,
So nimble is he,
His silvery powder he'll shake;
To windows he'll creep,
And while we're asleep,
Such wonderful pictures he'll make.

Across the grass
He'll merrily pass,
And change all its greenness to white;
Then home he will go,
And laugh, 'Ho! Ho! Ho!
What fun I have had in the night!'

Cecily Pike

Sir Nicketty Nox

Sir Nicketty Nox was an ancient knight,
So old was he that he'd lost his sight.
Blind as a mole and slim as a fox,
And dry as a stick was Sir Nicketty Nox.

His sword and buckler were old and cracked,
So was his charger and that's a fact.
Thin as a rake from head to hocks,
Was this rickety nag of Sir Nicketty Nox.

A wife he had and daughters three,
And all were old, as old could be.
They mended the shirts and darned the socks
Of that old antiquity, Nicketty Nox.

Sir Nicketty Nox would fly in a rage
If anyone tried to guess his age.
He'd mouth and mutter and tear his locks,
This very pernickety Nicketty Nox.

Hugh Chesterman

Mrs Moon

Mrs Moon
sitting up in the sky
Little old lady
rock-a-bye
with a ball of fading light
and silvery needles
knitting the night.

Roger McGough

If You Should Meet a Crocodile

If you should meet a crocodile,
Don't take a stick and poke him;
Ignore the welcome in his smile,
Be careful not to stroke him.

For as he sleeps upon the Nile,
He thinner gets and thinner;
And whene'er you meet a crocodile
He's ready for his dinner.

Anonymous

Way Down South

Way down south where bananas grow,
A grasshopper stepped on an elephant's toe.
The elephant said, with tears in his eyes,
'Pick on somebody your own size!'

Anonymous

The Hippopotamus

The huge hippopotamus hasn't a hair
on the back of his wrinkly hide;
he carried the bulk of his prominent hulk
rather loosely assembled inside.

The huge hippopotamus lives without care
at a slow philosophical pace,
as he wades in the mud with a thump and a thud
and a permanent grin on his face.

Jack Prelutsky

The Duck

Behold the duck.
It does not cluck.
A cluck it lacks.
It quacks.
It is specially fond
Of a puddle or pond.
When it dines or sups,
It bottoms ups.

Ogden Nash

The Balloon Man

He always comes on market days,
And holds balloons – a lovely bunch –
And in the market square he stays,
And never seems to think of lunch.

They're red and purple, blue and green,
And when it is a sunny day
Tho' carts and people get between
You see them shining far away.

And some are big and some are small,
All tied together with a string,
And if there is a wind at all
They tug and tug like anything.

Some day perhaps he'll let them go
And we shall see them sailing high,
And stand and watch them from below –
They *would* look pretty in the sky!

Rose Fyleman

Washing

What is all this washing about,
Every day, week in, week out?
From getting up till going to bed,
I'm tired of hearing the same thing said.
Whether I'm dirty or whether I'm not,
Whether the water is cold or hot,
Whether I like it or whether I don't,
Whether I will or whether I won't –
'Have you washed your hands, and washed your face?'
I seem to *live* in the washing place.

Whenever I go for a walk or ride,
As soon as I put my nose inside
The door again, there's someone there
With a sponge and soap, and a lot they care
If I have something better to do,
'Now wash your face and your fingers too.'

Before a meal is ever begun,
And after a meal is done,
It's time to turn on the waterspout.
Please, what *is* all this washing about?

John Drinkwater

The Witch

I saw her plucking cowslips,
And marked her where she stood:
She never knew I watched her
While hiding in the wood.

Her skirt was brightest crimson,
And black her steeple hat,
Her broomstick lay beside her –
I'm positive of that.

Her chin was sharp and pointed,
Her eyes were – I don't know –
For, when she turned towards me
I thought it best to go!

Percy H. Ilott

The Serpent

There was a Serpent who had to sing.
There was. There was.
He simply gave up Serpenting.
Because. Because.
He didn't like his Kind of Life;
He couldn't find a proper Wife;
He was a Serpent with a soul;
He got no Pleasure down his Hole.
And so, of course, he had to Sing,
And Sing he did, like Anything!
The Birds, they were, they were Astounded;
And various Measures Propounded
To stop the Serpent's awful Racket:
They bought a Drum. He wouldn't Whack it.
They sent – you always send – to Cuba
And got a most Commodious Tuba;
They got a Horn, they got a Flute
But Nothing would suit.
He said, 'Look, Birds, all this is futile:
I do *not* like to Bang or Tootle.'
And then he cut loose with a Horrible Note
That practically split the Top of his Throat.
'You see,' he said, with a Serpent's leer,
'I'm Serious about my Singing Career!'
And the Woods Resounded with many a Shriek
As the Birds flew off to the End of Next Week.

Theodore Roethke

He was a Rat

He was a rat, and she was a rat,
And down in one hole they did dwell,
And both were as black as a witch's cat,
And they loved each other well.

He had a tail, and she had a tail,
Both long and curling fine;
And each said, 'Yours is the finest tail
In the world, excepting mine!'

He smelt the cheese, and she smelt the cheese,
And they both pronounced it good;
And both remarked it would greatly add
To the charms of their daily food.

So he ventured out, and she ventured out,
And I saw them go with pain;
But what befell them I never can tell
For they never came back again.

Anonymous

The Frog and the Bird

By a quiet little stream on an old mossy log,
Looking very forlorn, sat a little green frog;
He'd a sleek speckled back, and two bright yellow eyes,
And when dining, selected the choicest of flies.

The sun was so hot he scarce opened his eyes,
Far too lazy to stir, let alone watch for flies,
He was nodding, and nodding, and almost asleep,
When a voice in the branches chirped: 'Froggie, cheep, cheep!'

'You'd better take care,' chirped the bird to the frog.
'In the water you'll be if you fall off that log.
Can't you see that the streamlet is up to the brim?'
Croaked the froggie, 'What odds! You forget I can swim.'

Then the froggie looked up at the bird perched so high
On a bough that to him seemed to reach to the sky;
So he croaked to the bird, 'If you fall, you will die!'
Chirped the birdie; 'What odds! You forget I can fly!'

Vera Hessey

The Dustman

When the shades of night are falling, and the sun
  goes down,
O! The Dustman comes a-creeping in from Shut-eye Town.
And he throws dust in the eyes of all the babies that
  he meets,
No matter where he finds them: in the house,
  or in the streets.
Then the babies' eyes grow heavy and the lids drop down,
When the Dustman comes a-creeping in from
  Shut-eye Town.

When mother lights the lamps and draws the curtains down
O! The Dustman comes a-creeping in from Shut-eye Town,
And the babies think the Dustman is as mean as he can be,
For he shuts their eyes at nightfall, just when they
  want to see.
But their little limbs are weary, for all they fret and frown,
When the Dustman comes a-creeping in from
  Shut-eye Town.

Anonymous

The Table and the Chair

Said the Table to the Chair,
'You can hardly be aware
How I suffer from the heat
And from the chilblains on my feet.
If we took a little walk,
We might have a little talk;
Pray let us take the air,'
Said the Table to the Chair.

Said the Chair unto the Table,
'Now, you know we are not able:
How foolishly you talk,
When you know we cannot walk!'
Said the Table with a sigh,
'It can do no harm to try.
I've as many legs as you;
Why can't we walk on two?'

So they both went slowly down,
And walked about the town
With a cheerful bumpy sound
As they toddled round and round;
And everybody cried,
As they hastened to their side,
'See! The Table and the Chair
Have come out to take the air!'

But in going down an alley
To a castle in a valley,
They completely lost their way,
And they wandered all the day;
Till, to see them safely back,
They paid a Ducky-quack,
And a Beetle and a Mouse,
Who took them to their house.

Then they whispered to each other,
'O delightful little brother,
What a lovely walk we've taken!
Let us dine on beans and bacon.'
So the Ducky and the leetle
Browny-Mousy and the Beetle
Dined and danced upon their heads
Till they toddled to their beds.

Edward Lear

Fairies

There are fairies at the bottom of our garden!
It's not so very, very far away;
You pass the gardener's shed and you just keep straight ahead –
I do so hope they've really come to stay.
There's a little wood, with moss in it and beetles,
And a little stream that quietly runs through;
You wouldn't think they'd dare to come merry-making there –
Well, they do.

There are fairies at the bottom of our garden!
They often have a dance on summer nights;
The butterflies and bees make a lovely little breeze,
And the rabbits stand about and hold the lights.
Did you know that they could sit upon the moonbeams
And pick a little star to make a fan?
And dance away up there in the middle of the air?
Well, they can.

There are fairies at the bottom of our garden!
You cannot think how beautiful they are;
They all stand up and sing when the Fairy Queen and King
Come gently floating down upon their car.
The King is *very* proud and very handsome;
The Queen – now can you guess who that could be
(She's a little girl all day, but at night she steals away)?
Well – it's Me!

Rose Fyleman

Father William

'You are old, Father William,' the young man said,
'And your hair has become very white;
And yet you incessantly stand on your head –
Do you think, at your age, it is right?'

'In my youth,' Father William replied to his son,
'I feared it might injure my brain;
But now that I'm perfectly sure I have none,
Why, I do it again and again.'

'You are old,' said the youth, 'as I mentioned before,
And have grown most uncommonly fat;
Yet you turned a back somersault in at the door –
Pray, what is the reason of that?'

'In my youth,' said the sage, as he shook his grey locks,
'I kept all my limbs very supple.
By the use of this ointment – one shilling the box –
Allow me to sell you a couple?'

'You are old,' said the youth, 'and your jaws are too weak
For anything tougher than suet;
Yet you finished the goose, with the bones and the beak –
Pray, how did you manage to do it?'

'In my youth,' said his father, 'I took to the law,
And argued each case with my wife;
And the muscular strength that it gave to my jaw,
Has lasted the rest of my life.'

'You are old,' said the youth, 'one would hardly suppose
That your eye was as steady as ever;
Yet you balanced an eel on the end of your nose –
What made you so awfully clever?'

'I have answered three questions and that is enough,'
Said his father. 'Don't give yourself airs!
Do you think I can listen all day to such stuff!
Be off, or I'll kick you downstairs!'

Lewis Carroll

Winter the Huntsman

Through his iron glades
Rides Winter the Huntsman.
All colour fades
As his horn is heard sighing.

Far through the forest
His wild hooves crash and thunder
Till many a mighty branch
Is torn asunder.

As the red reynard creeps
To his hole near the river,
The copper leaves fall
And the bare trees shiver.

As night creeps from the ground,
Hides each tree from its brother,
And each dying sound
Reveals yet another.

Is it Winter the Huntsman
Who gallops through his iron glades,
Cracking his cruel whip
To the gathering shades?

Osbert Sitwell

The Traveller

Old man, old man, sitting on the stile,
Your boots are worn, your clothes are torn,
Tell us why you smile.

Children, children, what silly things you are!
My boots are worn and my clothes are torn
Because I've walked so far.

Old man, old man, where have you walked from?
Your legs are bent, your breath is spent.
Which way did you come?

Children, children, when you're old and lame,
When your legs are bent and your breath is spent
You'll know the way I came.

Old man, old man, have you far to go
Without a friend to your journey's end,
And why are you so slow?

Children, children, I do the best I may.
I meet a friend at my journey's end
With whom you'll meet some day.

Old man, old man, sitting on the stile,
How do you know which way to go,
And why is it you smile?

Children, children, butter should be spread,
Floors should be swept and promises kept,
And you should be in bed!

Raymond Wilson

Nothing

He thought he heard
A footstep on the stair,
'It's nothing,' he said to himself,
'Nothing is there.'
He thought then he heard
A snuffling in the hall,
'It's nothing,' he said again,
'Nothing at all.'
But he didn't open the door
In case he found nothing
Standing there,
On foot or tentacle or paw.
Timidly quiet he kept to his seat
While nothing stalked the house
On great big feet.
It was strange though
And he'd noticed this
When on his own before,
Nothing stalked throughout the house
But never through his door.
The answer he thought
Was very plain. It was because there was
Nothing there –
Again!

Julie Holder

The Hag

The Hag is astride,
This night for to ride;
The Devil and she together:
Through thick and through thin,
Now out, and then in,
Though ne'er so foul be the weather.

A Thorn or a Burr
She takes for a Spur:
With a lash of a Bramble she rides now,
Through Brakes and through Briars,
O'er Ditches and Mires,
She follows the Spirit that guides now.

No Beast, for his food,
Dares now range the wood;
But hush'd in his lair he lies lurking;
While mischiefs by these,
On Land and on Seas,
At noon of Night are a-working.

The storm will arise,
And trouble the skies;
This night, and more Tomb
Affrighted shall come,
Called out by the clap of the Thunder.

Robert Herrick

The Moon

The moon has a face like the clock in the hall;
She shines on thieves and on the garden wall,
On streets and fields and harbour quays,
And birdies asleep in the forks of the trees.

The squalling cat and the squeaking mouse,
The howling dog by the door of the house,
The bat that lies in bed at noon,
All love to be out by the light of the moon.

But all of the things that belong to the day
Cuddle to sleep to be out of her way;
And flowers and children close their eyes
Till up in the morning the sun shall rise.

Robert Louis Stevenson

The Witches' Call

Come, witches, come, on your hithering brooms!
The moorland is dark and still
Over the church and the churchyard tombs
To the oakwood under the hill.

Come through the mist and the wandering cloud,
Fly with the crescent moon;
Come where the witches and warlocks crowd,
Come soon ... soon!

Leave your room with its shadowy cat,
Your cauldron over the hearth;
Seize your cloak and pointed hat,
Come by the witches' path.
Float from the earth like a rising bird,
Stream through the darkening air,
Come at the sound of our secret word,
Come to the witches' lair!

Clive Sansom

Past, Present, Future

Tell me, tell me, smiling child,
What the past is like to thee?
'An Autumn evening soft and mild
With a wind that sighs mournfully.'

Tell me, what is the present hour?
'A green and flowery spray
Where a young bird sits gathering its power
To mount and fly away.'

And what is the future, happy one?
'A sea beneath a cloudless sun;
A mighty, glorious, dazzling sea
Stretching into infinity.'

Emily Brontë

Where Lies the Land

Where lies the land to which the ship would go?
Far, far ahead, is all her seamen know.
And where the land she travels from? Away,
Far, far behind, is all that they can say.

On sunny morns upon the deck's smooth face,
Linked arm in arm, how pleasant here to pace;
Or o'er the stern reclining, watch below
The foaming wake far widening as we go.

On stormy nights when wild north-westers rave,
How proud a thing to fight with wind and wave!
The dripping sailor on the reeling mast
Exults to bear, and scorns to wish it past.

Where lies the land to which the ship would go?
Far, far ahead, is all her seamen know.
And where the land she travels from? Away,
Far, far behind, is all that they can say.

A. H. Clough

The Butterfly's Ball

Come, take up your hats, and away let us haste
To the butterfly's ball and the grasshopper's feast;
The trumpeter gadfly has summoned the crew,
And revels are now only waiting for you.

On the smooth shaven grass, by the side of the wood,
Beneath a broad oak that for ages has stood,
See the children of earth, and the tenants of air,
For an evening's amusement together repair.

And there came the beetle so blind and so black,
Who carried the emmet, his friend, on his back;
And there was the gnat and the dragonfly too,
With all their relations, green, orange and blue.

And there came the moth in his plumage of down,
And the hornet in jacket of yellow and brown,
Who with him the wasp his companion did bring,
But they promised that evening to lay by their sting.

And the sly little dormouse crept out of his hole,
And led to the feast his blind brother the mole,
And the snail, with his horns peeping out from his shell,
Came from a great distance – the length of an ell.

A mushroom their table, and on it was laid
A water-dock leaf, which a tablecloth made;
The viands were various, to each of their taste,
And the bee brought his honey to crown the repast.

There, close on his haunches, so solemn and wise,
The frog from a corner looked up to the skies;

And the squirrel, well pleased such diversions to see,
Sat cracking his nuts overhead in a tree.

Then out came the spider, with fingers so fine,
To show his dexterity on the tight line;
From one branch to another his cobwebs he slung,
Then, quick as an arrow, he darted along.

But just in the middle, oh! Shocking to tell!
From his rope in an instant poor Harlequin fell;
Yet he touched not the ground, but with talons outspread
Hung suspended in air at the end of a thread.

Then the grasshopper came with a jerk and a spring,
Very long was his leg, though by short was his wing;
He took but three leaps, and was soon out of sight,
Then chirped his own praises the rest of the night.

With step so majestic, the snail did advance,
And promised the gazers a minuet to dance;
But they laughed so loud that he pulled in his head,
And went in his own little chamber to bed.

Then as evening gave way to the shadows of night
Their watchman, the glow-worm, came out with his light;
Then home let us hasten while yet we can see,
For no watchman is waiting for you and for me.

William Roscoe

Meg Merrilees

Old Meg she was a Gipsy,
And liv'd upon the moors:
Her bed it was the brown heath turf,
And her house was out of doors.

Her apples were swart blackberries,
Her currants pods o' broom;
Her wine was dew o' the wild white rose,
Her book a churchyard tomb.

Her Brothers were the craggy hills,
Her Sisters larchen trees-
Alone with her great family
She liv'd as she did please.

No breakfast had she many a morn,
No dinner many a noon,
And 'stead of supper she would stare
Full hard against the Moon.

But every morn of woodbine fresh
She made her garlanding,
And every night the dark glen Yew
She wove, and she would sing.

And with her fingers old and brown,
She plaited Mats o' Rushes,
And gave them to the Cottagers
She met among the Bushes.

Old Meg was brave as Margaret Queen
And tall as Amazon:
An old red blanket cloak she wore;
A chip-hat she had on.
God rest her aged bones somewhere-
She died full long agone!

John Keats

My Shadow

I have a little shadow that goes in and out with me,
And what can be the use of him is more than I can see.
He is very, very like me from the heels up to the head;
And I see him jump before me, when I jump into my bed.

The funniest thing about him is the way he likes to grow,
Not at all like proper children, which is always very slow.
For he sometimes shoots up taller like an india-rubber ball,
And he sometimes gets so little that there's none of him at all.

He hasn't got a notion of how children ought to play,
And can only make a fool of me in every sort of way.
He stays so close beside me, he's a coward you can see;
I'd think shame to stick to Nursie as that shadow sticks to me!

One morning, very early, before the sun was up,
I rose and found the shining dew on every buttercup,
But my lazy little shadow, like an arrant sleepy-head,
Had stayed at home behind me and was fast asleep in bed.

Robert Louis Stevenson

Johnny Crow's Garden

Johnny Crow
Would dig and sow
Till he made a little Garden.

And the Lion
Had a green and yellow Tie on
In Johnny Crow's Garden.

And the Rat
Wore a Feather in his Hat
But the Bear had nothing to wear
In Johnny Crow's Garden.

So the Ape
Took his Measure with a Tape
In Johnny Crow's Garden.

Then the Crane
Was caught in the Rain
In Johnny Crow's Garden.

And the Beaver
Was afraid he had a Fever
But the Goat said,

'It's nothing but his Throat,'
In Johnny Crow's Garden.

And the Pig
Danced a Jig
In Johnny Crow's Garden.

Then the Stork gave a Philosophic Talk
Till the Hippopotami
Said: 'Ask no further "What am I?"'
While the elephant
Said something quite irrelevant
In Johnny Crow's garden.

And the goose –
Well,
The goose was a goose
In Johnny Crow's garden.

And the mouse
Built himself a little house
Where the cat
Sat down beside the mat
In Johnny Crow's garden.

And the owl
Was a funny old fowl
And the fox
Put them all in the stocks
In Johnny Crow's garden.

But Johnny Crow
He let them go
And they all sat down
To their dinner in a row
In Johnny Crow's garden!

L. Leslie Brooke

Silver

Slowly, silently, now the moon
Walks the night in her silver shoon;
This way, and that, she peers, and sees
Silver fruit upon silver trees;
One by one the casements catch
Her beams beneath the silvery thatch;
Couched in his kennel like a log,
With paws of silver sleeps the dog;
From their shadowy cote the white breasts peep
Of doves in a silver-feathered sleep;
A harvest mouse goes scampering by,
With silver paws, and silver eye;
And moveless fish in the water gleam,
By silver reeds in a silver stream.

Walter de la Mare

The Wind

I saw you toss the kites on high
And blow the birds about the sky;
And all around I heard you pass,
Like ladies' skirts across the grass –
O wind, a-blowing all day long,
O wind, that sings so loud a song!

I saw the different things you did,
But always you yourself you hid.
I felt you push, I heard you call,
I could not see yourself at all –
O wind, a-blowing all day long,
O wind, that sings so loud a song!

O you that are so strong and cold,
O blower, are you young or old?
Are you a beast of field and tree,
Or just a stronger child than me?
O wind, a-blowing all day long,
O wind, that sings so loud a song!

Robert Louis Stevenson

The Fly-Away Horse

Oh, a wonderful horse is the Fly-Away Horse,
Perhaps you have seen him before.
Perhaps, while you slept, his shadow has swept
Through the moonlight that floats on the floor.
For it's only at night, when the stars twinkle bright,
That the Fly-Away Horse, with a neigh
And a pull at his rein and a toss of his mane,
Is up on his heels and away!
The Moon in the sky,
As he gallopeth by,
Cries, 'Oh! What a marvellous sight!'
And the Stars in dismay
Hide their faces away
In the lap of old Grandmother Night.

It is yonder, out yonder, the Fly-Away Horse
Speedeth ever and ever away,
Over meadows and lanes, over mountains and plains,
Over streamlets that sing at their play.
And over the sea like a ghost sweepeth he,
While the ships they go sailing below,
And he speedeth so fast that the men at the mast
Adjudge him some portent of woe.
'What ho, there!' they cry,

As he flourishes by
With a whisk of his beautiful tail.
And the fish in the sea
Are as scared as can be,
From the nautilus up to the whale!

And the Fly-Away Horse seeks those far-away lands
You little folk dream of at night,
Where candy-trees grow, and honey-brooks flow,
And cornfields with popcorn are white.
And the beasts in the wood are ever so good
To children who visit them there,
What glory astride of a lion to ride,
Or to wrestle around with a bear!
The monkeys they say,
'Come on, let us play,'
And they frisk in the coconut trees.
While the parrots that cling
To the peanut-vines, sing
Or converse with comparative ease!

Off! Scamper to bed, you shall ride him tonight!
For, as soon as you've fallen asleep,
With jubilant neigh he shall bear you away
Over forest and hillside and deep!
But tell us, my dear, all you see and you hear
In those beautiful lands over there,
Where the Fly-Away Horse wings his far-away course
With the wee one consigned to his care.
Then Grandma will cry
In amazement, 'Oh, my!'
And she'll think it could never be so.
And only we two
Shall know it is true.
You and I, little precious, shall know!

Eugene Field

The Tiger

Tiger! Tiger! Burning bright
In the forests of the night,
What immortal hand or eye
Could frame thy fearful symmetry?

In what distant deeps or skies
Burnt the fire of thine eyes?
On what wings dare he aspire?
What the hand dare seize the fire?

And what shoulder, and what art
Could twist the sinews of thy heart?
And, when thy heart began to beat,
What dread hand forged thy dread feet?

What the hammer? What the chain?
In what furnace was thy brain?
What the anvil? What dread grasp
Dare its deadly terrors clasp?

When the stars threw down their spears,
And watered heaven with their tears,
Did He smile His work to see?
Did He who made the lamb make thee?

Tiger! Tiger! Burning bright
In the forests of the night,
What immortal hand or eye
Could frame thy fearful symmetry?

William Blake

The Night will Never Stay

The night will never stay,
The night will still go by,
Though with a million stars
You pin it to the sky;
Though you bind it with the blowing wind
And buckle it with the moon,
The night will slip away
Like sorrow or a tune.

Eleanor Farjeon

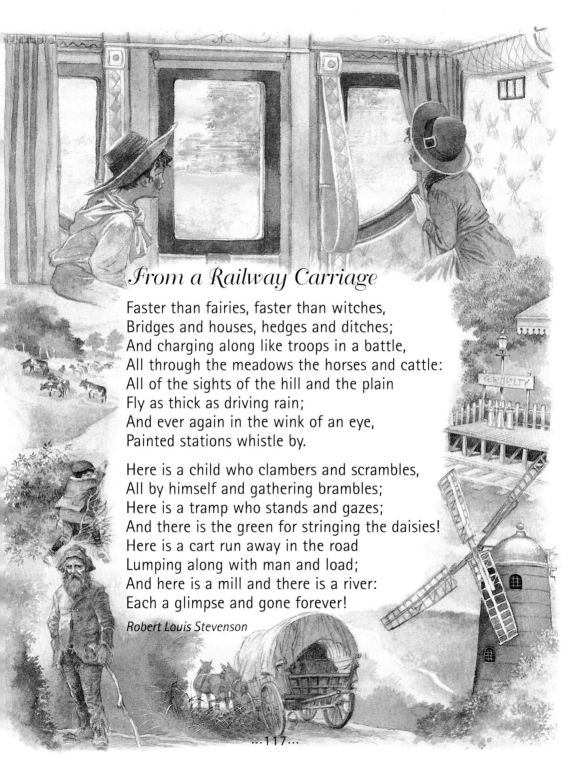

From a Railway Carriage

Faster than fairies, faster than witches,
Bridges and houses, hedges and ditches;
And charging along like troops in a battle,
All through the meadows the horses and cattle:
All of the sights of the hill and the plain
Fly as thick as driving rain;
And ever again in the wink of an eye,
Painted stations whistle by.

Here is a child who clambers and scrambles,
All by himself and gathering brambles;
Here is a tramp who stands and gazes;
And there is the green for stringing the daisies!
Here is a cart run away in the road
Lumping along with man and load;
And here is a mill and there is a river:
Each a glimpse and gone forever!

Robert Louis Stevenson

My Dog, Spot

I have a white dog
Whose name is Spot,
And he's sometimes white
And he's sometimes not.
But whether he's white,
Or whether he's not,
There's a patch on his ear
That makes him Spot.

He has a tongue
That is long and pink,
And he lolls it out
When he wants to think.
He seems to think most
When the weather is hot
He's a wise sort of dog,
Is my dog, Spot.

He likes a bone
And he likes a ball,
But he doesn't care
For a cat at all.
He waggles his tail
And he knows what's what,
So I'm glad that he's my dog,
My dog, Spot.

Rodney Bennett

I Wandered Lonely as a Cloud

I wandered lonely as a cloud
That floats on high o'er vales and hills,
When all at once I saw a crowd,
A host of golden daffodils;
Beside the lake, beneath the trees,
Fluttering and dancing in the breeze.

Continuous as the stars that shine
And twinkle on the Milky Way,
They stretched in never-ending line
Along the margin of a bay:
Ten thousand saw I at a glance,
Tossing their heads in sprightly dance.

The waves beside them danced; but they
Out-did the sparkling waves in glee:
A poet could not but be gay,
In such jocund company:
I gazed – and gazed – but little thought
What wealth the show to me had brought.

For oft, when on my couch I lie
In vacant or in pensive mood,
They flash upon that inward eye
Which is the bliss of solitude;
And then my heart with pleasure fills,
And dances with the daffodils.

William Wordsworth

The Owl

When cats run home and light is come,
And dew is cold upon the ground,
And the far-off stream is dumb,
And the whirring sail goes round,
And the whirring sail goes round;
Alone and warming his five wits,
The white owl in the belfry sits.

When merry milkmaids click the latch,
And rarely smells the new-mown hay,
And the cock hath sung beneath the thatch
Twice or thrice his roundelay,
Twice or thrice his roundelay;
Alone and warming his five wits,
The white owl in the belfry sits.

Alfred, Lord Tennyson

The Wind

Someone tapped at the window pane
    A little while ago.
Someone runs around the house,
    And whistles loud and low.
Someone shakes the garden gate,
    And climbs the garden wall.
Yet when I say: 'Who's that out there?'
    It's nobody at all.
He's calling down the chimney now,
    With quite a noisy roar;
He's piping through the keyhole,
    And he's knocking on the door.
'Come in! Come in!' But no one comes.
    I peep into the hall.
And though I feel a puff of wind,
    There's no one there at all.

John Lea

The Song of Mr Toad

The world has held great Heroes,
  As history books have showed;
But never a name to go down to fame
  Compared with that of Toad!

The clever men at Oxford
  Know all there is to be knowed,
But they none of them know one half as much
  As intelligent Mr Toad!

The animals sat in the Ark and cried,
  Their tears in torrents flowed.
Who was it said, 'There's land ahead?'
  Encouraging Mr Toad!

The Army all saluted
  As they marched along the road.
Was it the King? Or Kitchener?
  No. It was Mr Toad!

The Queen and her Ladies-in-waiting
  Sat at the window and sewed.
She cried, 'Look! Who's that *handsome* man?'
  They answered, 'Mr Toad.'

Kenneth Grahame

Someone

Someone came knocking
At my wee, small door;
Someone came knocking,
I'm sure, sure, sure;
I listened, I opened,
I looked to left and right,
But nought there was a-stirring
In the still, dark night.
Only the busy beetle
Tap-tapping in the wall,
Only from the forest
The screech-owl's call,
Only the cricket whistling
While the dewdrops fall,
So I know not who came knocking,
At all, at all, at all.

Walter de la Mare

The Fly

How large unto the tiny fly
Must little things appear!
A rosebud like a feather bed
Its prickle like a spear;

A dewdrop like a looking-glass,
A hair like golden wire;
The smallest grain of mustard-seed
As fierce as coals of fire;

A loaf of bread, a lofty hill;
A wasp, a cruel leopard;
And specks of salt as bright to see
As lambkins to a shepherd.

Walter de la Mare

Fairy Story

I went into the wood one day
And there I walked and lost my way

When it was so dark I could not see
A little creature came to me

He said I could sing a song
The time would not be very long

But first I must let him hold my hand tight
Or else the wood would give me a fright

I sang a song, he let me go
But now I am home again there is nobody I know.

Stevie Smith

If Pigs Could Fly

If pigs could fly, I'd fly a pig
To foreign countries small and big.
To Italy and Spain,
To Austria, where cowbells ring,
To Germany, where people sing,
And then come home again.

I'd see the Ganges and the Nile.
I'd visit Madagascar's isle,
And Persia and Peru.
People would say they'd never seen
So odd, so strange an air-machine
As that on which I flew.

Why, everyone would raise a shout
To see his trotters and his snout
Come floating from the sky.
And I would be a famous star
Well known in countries near and far.
If only pigs could fly!

James Reeves

Windy Nights

Whenever the moon and stars are set,
Whenever the wind is high,
All night long in the dark and wet,
A man goes riding by.
Late in the night when the fires are out,
Why does he gallop and gallop about?

Whenever the trees are crying aloud,
And ships are tossed at sea,
By on the highway, low and loud,
By at the gallop goes he.
By at the gallop he goes, and then
By he comes back at the gallop again.

Robert Louis Stevenson

The Walrus and the Carpenter

The sun was shining on the sea,
Shining with all his might.
He did his very best to make
The billows smooth and bright,
And this was odd, because it was
The middle of the night.

The moon was shining sulkily,
Because she thought the sun
Had got no business to be there
After the day was done.
'It's very rude of him,' she said,
'To come and spoil the fun!'

The sea was wet as wet could be,
The sands were dry as dry.
You could not see a cloud, because
No cloud was in the sky.
No birds were flying overhead,
There were no birds to fly.

The Walrus and the Carpenter
Were walking close at hand.
They wept like anything to see
Such quantities of sand.
'If this were only cleared away,'
They said, 'it *would* be grand!'

'If seven maids with seven mops
Swept it for half a year,
Do you suppose,' the Walrus said,

'That they would get it clear?'
'I doubt it,' said the Carpenter,
And shed a bitter tear.

'O, Oysters come and walk with us!'
The Walrus did beseech.
'A pleasant walk, a pleasant talk,
Along the briny beach.
We cannot do with more than four,
To give a hand to each.'

The eldest Oyster looked at him,
But never a word he said.
The eldest Oyster winked his eye,
And shook his heavy head,
Meaning to say he did not choose
To leave the oyster-bed.

But four young Oysters hurried up,
All eager for the treat.
Their coats were brushed, their faces washed,
Their shoes were clean and neat,
And this was odd, because, as you know,
They hadn't any feet.

Four other Oysters followed them,
And yet another four.
And thick and fast they came at last,
And more, and more, and more;
All hopping through the frothy waves,
And scrambling to the shore.

The Walrus and the Carpenter
Walked on a mile or so,
And then they rested on a rock
Conveniently low,
And all the little Oysters stood
And waited in a row.

'The time has come,' the Walrus said,
'To talk of many things,
Of shoes – and ships – and sealing wax –
Of cabbages – and kings –
And why the sea is boiling hot –
And whether pigs have wings.'

'But wait a bit,' the Oysters cried,
'Before we have our chat.
For some of us are out of breath,
And all of us are fat!'
'No hurry,' said the Carpenter.
They thanked him much for that.

'A loaf of bread,' the Walrus said,
'Is what we chiefly need;
Pepper and vinegar besides
Are very good indeed.
Now if you're ready, Oysters dear,
We can begin to feed.'

'But not on us!' the Oysters cried,
Turning a little blue.
'After such kindness, that would be
A dismal thing to do!'
'The night is fine,' the Walrus said.
'Do you admire the view?'

'It was so kind of you to come!
And you are very nice!'

The Carpenter said nothing but,
'Cut us another slice.
I wish you were not quite so deaf,
I've had to ask you twice!'

'It seems a shame,' the Walrus said,
'To play them such a trick.
After we've brought them out so far,
And made them trot so quick!'
The Carpenter said nothing but,
'The butter's spread too thick!'

'I weep for you,' the Walrus said,
'I deeply sympathise.'
With sobs and tears he sorted out
Those of the largest size,
Holding his pocket handkerchief
Before his streaming eyes.

'O, Oysters,' said the Carpenter,
'You've had a pleasant run!
Shall we be trotting home again?'
But answer came there none,
And this was scarcely odd, because
They'd eaten every one.

Lewis Carroll

The Sugar-Plum Tree

Have you heard of the Sugar-Plum Tree?
'Tis a marvel of great renown!
It blooms on the shores of the Lollipop Sea
In the garden of Shut-Eye Town;
The fruit that it bears is so wondrously sweet
(As those who have tasted it say)
That good little children have only to eat
Of that fruit to be happy next day.

When you've got to the tree, you would have a hard time
To capture the fruit which I sing;
The tree is so tall that no person could climb
To the bough where the sugar-plums swing!
But up in that tree sits a chocolate cat,
And a gingerbread dog prowls below,
And this is the way you contrive to get at
Those sugar-plums tempting you so.

You say but the word to that gingerbread dog
And he barks with such terrible zest
That the chocolate cat is at once all agog,
As her swelling proportions attest.
And the chocolate cat goes cavorting around
From this leafy limb unto that,
And the sugar-plums tumble, of course, to the ground.
Hurrah for the chocolate cat!

There are marshmallows, gumdrops, and peppermint canes
With stripings of scarlet or gold,
And you carry away of the treasure that rains
As much as your apron can hold!
So come, little child, cuddle closer to me
In your dainty white nightcap and gown,
And I'll rock you away to that Sugar-Plum Tree
In the garden of Shut-Eye Town.

Eugene Field

Frutta di Mare

I am a sea shell flung
Up from the ancient sea;
Now I lie here, among
Roots of a tamarisk tree;
No one listens to me.

I sing to myself all day
In a husky voice, quite low,
Things the great fishes say
And you must need to know;
All night I sing just so.

But lift me from the ground,
And hearken at my rim;
Only your sorrow's sound
Amazed, perplexed and dim,
Comes coiling to the brim;

For what the wise whales ponder
Awaking out from sleep,
The key to all your wonder,
The answers of the deep,
These to myself I keep.

Geoffrey Scott

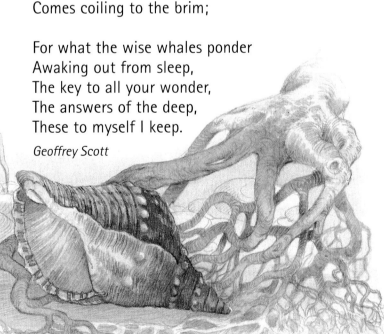

Eldorado

Gaily bedight,
A gallant knight,
In sunshine and in shadow,
Had journeyed long,
Singing a song,
In search of Eldorado.

But he grew old,
This knight so bold
And o'er his heart a shadow
Fell, as he found
No spot of ground
That looked like Eldorado.

And, as his strength
Failed him at length,
He met a pilgrim shadow.
'Shadow,' said he,
'Where can it be,
This land of Eldorado?'

'Over the Mountains
Of the Moon,
Down the Valley of the Shadow,
Ride, boldly ride,'
The shadow replied,
'If you seek for Eldorado!'

Edgar Allan Poe

My Mother Said

My mother said I never should
Play with the Gypsies in the wood.
If I did, she would say,
'Naughty girl to disobey.
Your hair shan't curl
And your shoes shan't shine,
You Gypsy girl,
You shan't be mine.'

And my father said that if I did
He'd rap my head with the teapot lid.
The wood was dark, the grass was green,
In came Sally with a tambourine.
I went to the sea, no ship to get across.
I paid ten shillings for a blind white horse.
I got up on his back and was off in a crack.
Sally, tell my mother I shall never come back.

Anonymous

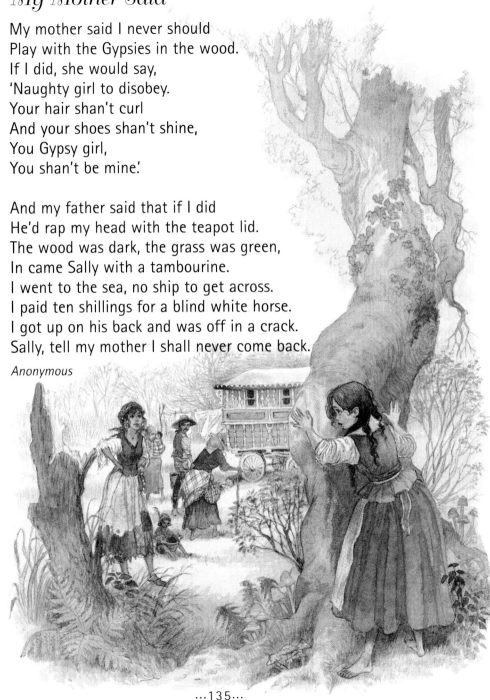

Hallowe'en

This is the night when witches fly
On their whizzing broomsticks through the wintry sky;
Steering up the pathway where the stars are strewn,
They stretch skinny fingers to the waking moon.

This is the night when old wives tell
Strange and creepy stories, tales of charm and spell;
Peering at the pictures flaming in the fire,
They wait for whispers from a ghostly choir.

This is the night when angels go
In and out of houses, winging o'er the snow;
Clearing out the demons from the countryside
They make it new and ready for Christmastide.

Leonard Clark

The Dark House

In a dark, dark wood, there was a dark, dark house,
In that dark, dark house, there was a dark, dark room,
And in that dark, dark room, there was a dark, dark cupboard,
And in that dark, dark cupboard, there was a dark, dark shelf,
And on that dark, dark shelf, there was a dark, dark box,
And in that dark, dark box, there was a GHOST!

Anonymous

The Rainbow Fairies

Two little clouds, one summer's day,
Went flying through the sky.
They went so fast they bumped their heads,
And both began to cry.

Old Father Sun looked out and said,
'Oh, never mind, my dears,
I'll send my little fairy folk
To dry your falling tears.'

One fairy came in violet,
And one wore indigo,
In blue, green, yellow, orange, red,
They made a pretty row.

They wiped the cloud-tears all away,
And then from out the sky,
Upon the line the sunbeams made,
They hung their gowns to dry.

Anonymous

The Little Things that Happen

The Little Things That Happen
Are tucked into your mind,
And come again to greet you
(Or most of them you'll find).

Through many little doorways,
Of which you keep the keys,
They crowd into your thinking–
We call them Memories.

But some of them are rovers
And wander off and get
So lost, the keys grow rusty,
And that means – you forget.

But some stay ever near you;
You'll find they never rove–
The keys are always shining–
Those are the things you love.

Marjorie Wilson

A Night with a Wolf

High up on the lonely mountains,
Where the wild men watched and waited,
Wolves in the forest, and bears in the bush,
And I on my path belated.

The rain and the night together
Came down, and the wind came after,
Bending the props of the pine-tree roof,
And snapping many a rafter.

I crept along in the darkness,
Stunned, and bruised, and blinded,
Crept to a fir with thick-set boughs,
And a sheltering rock behind it.

There, from the blowing and raining,
Crouching, I sought to hide me.
Something rustled, two green eyes shone,
And a wolf lay down beside me!

His wet fur pressed against me,
Each of us warmed the other.
Each of us felt, in the stormy dark,
That beast and man were brother.

And when the falling forest
No longer crashed in warning,
Each of us went from our hiding place
Forth in the wild, wet morning.

Bayard Taylor

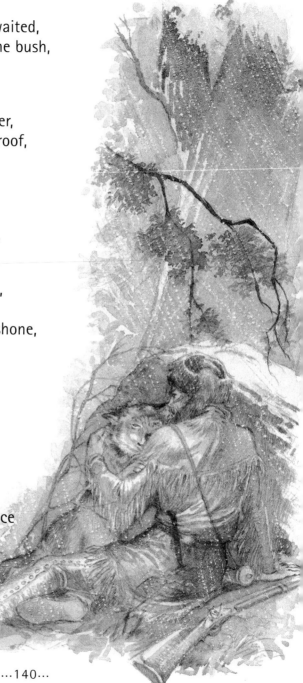

A Kitten

He's nothing much but fur
And two round eyes of blue,
He has a giant purr
And a midget mew.

He darts and pats the air,
He starts and pricks his ear,
When there is nothing there
For him to see and hear.

He runs around in rings
But why we cannot tell.
With sideways leap he springs
At things invisible –

Then halfway through a leap
His startled eyeballs close,
And he drops off to sleep
With one paw on his nose.

Eleanor Farjeon

The Owl and the Pussy-Cat

The Owl and the Pussy-Cat went to sea
In a beautiful pea-green boat,
They took some honey and plenty of money,
Wrapped up in a five-pound note.
The Owl looked up to the stars above,
And sang to a small guitar,
'O lovely Pussy! O Pussy, my love,
What a beautiful Pussy you are,
You are,
You are!
What a beautiful Pussy you are!'

Pussy said to the Owl, 'You elegant fowl!
How charmingly sweet you sing!
O let us be married! Too long we have tarried,
But what shall we do for a ring?'
They sailed away, for a year and a day,
To the land where the Bong-Tree grows,
And there in a wood a Piggy-wig stood,
With a ring at the end of his nose,
His nose,
His nose,
With a ring at the end of his nose.

'Dear Pig, are you willing to sell for one shilling
Your ring?' Said the Piggy, 'I will!'
So they took it away, and were married next day
By the Turkey who lives on the hill.
They dined on mince, and slices of quince,
Which they ate with a runcible spoon.
And hand in hand, on the edge of the sand,
They danced by the light of the moon,
The moon,
The moon,
They danced by the light of the moon.
Edward Lear

The White Seagull

The white seagull, the wild seagull!
A joyful bird is he,
As he lies like a cradled thing at rest
In the arms of a sunny sea!
The little waves wash to and fro,
And the little white gull lies asleep
As the fisher's boat with breeze and tide,
Goes merrily over the deep.
The ship, with her sails set, goes by
And her people stand to note
How the seagull sits on the rocking waves,
As still as an anchored boat.
The sea is fresh and the sea is fair,
And the sky is calm overhead
And the seagull lies on the deep, deep sea,
Like a king in his royal bed!

Mary Howitt

The Robin

When up aloft
I fly and fly,
I see in pools
The shining sky,
And a happy bird
Am I, am I!

When I descend
Toward the brink,
I stand and look
And stop and drink
And bathe my wings,
And chink, and prink.

When winter frost
Makes earth as steel,
I search and search
But find no meal,
And most unhappy
Then I feel.

But when it lasts
And snows still fall,
I get to feel
No grief at all,
For I turn to a cold, stiff
Feather ball!

Thomas Hardy

Answer to a Child's Question

Do you ask what the birds say?
The sparrow, the dove, the linnet
And the thrush say, 'I love and I love!'
In the winter they're silent, the wind is so strong,
What it says, I don't know, but it sings a loud song.
But green leaves, and blossoms,
And sunny warm weather,
And singing, and loving all come back together.
But the lark is so brimful of gladness and love,
The green fields below him, the blue sky above,
That he sings, and he sings, and forever sings he,
'I love my Love, and my Love loves me!'

Samuel Taylor Coleridge

The Sound of the Wind

The wind has such a rainy sound
Moaning through the town.
The sea has such a windy sound,
Will the ships go down?

The apples in the orchard
Tumble from their tree.
Oh will the ships go down, go down,
In the windy sea?

Christina Rossetti

The Little Wee Man

As I was walking all alone
Between a river and a wall,
There I saw a little wee man
I'd never seen a man so small.

His legs were barely a finger long,
His shoulders wide as fingers three.
Light and springing was his step,
And he stood lower than my knee.

He lifted a stone six feet high,
He lifted it up to his right knee,
Above his chest, above his head,
And flung it as far as I could see.

'O,' said I, 'how strong you are!
I wonder where your home can be?'
'Down the green valley there.
O will you come with me and see?'

So on we ran, and away we rode,
Until we came to his bonny home.
The roof was made of beaten gold,
The floor was made of crystal stone.

Pipers were playing, ladies dancing,
Four-and-twenty ladies gay.
And as they danced they were singing,
'Our little wee man's been long away.'

Ian Serraillier

A Fairy went A-marketing

A fairy went a-marketing –
She bought a little fish;
She put it in a crystal bowl
Upon a golden dish.
An hour she sat in wonderment
And watched its silver gleam,
And then she gently took it up
And slipped it in a stream.

A fairy went a-marketing –
She bought a coloured bird;
It sang the sweetest, shrillest song
That ever she had heard,
She sat beside its painted cage
And listened half the day,
And then she opened wide the door
And let it fly away.

A fairy went a-marketing –
She bought a winter gown
All stitched about with gossamer
And lined with thistledown.
She wore it all the afternoon
With prancing and delight,
Then gave it to a little frog
To keep him warm at night.

A fairy went a-marketing –
She bought a gentle mouse
To take her tiny messages,
To keep her little house.
All day she kept its busy feet
Pit-patting to and fro,
And then she kissed its silken ears,
Thanked it and let it go.

Rose Fyleman

The House That Jack Built

This is the house that Jack built.

This is the malt
That lay in the house that Jack built.

This is the rat,
That ate the malt
That lay in the house that Jack built.

This is the cat,
That killed the rat,
That ate the malt
That lay in the house that Jack built.

This is the dog,
That worried the cat,
That killed the rat,
That ate the malt
That lay in the house that Jack built.

This is the cow with the crumpled horn,
That tossed the dog,
That worried the cat,
That killed the rat,
That ate the malt
That lay in the house that Jack built.

This is the maiden all forlorn,
That milked the cow with the crumpled horn,
That tossed the dog,
That worried the cat,
That killed the rat,
That ate the malt
That lay in the house that Jack built.

This is the man all tattered and torn,
That kissed the maiden all forlorn,
That milked the cow with the crumpled horn,
That tossed the dog,
That worried the cat,
That killed the rat,
That ate the malt
That lay in the house that Jack built.

This is the priest all shaven and shorn,
That married the man all tattered and torn,
That kissed the maiden all forlorn,
That milked the cow with the crumpled horn,
That tossed the dog,
That worried the cat,
That killed the rat,
That ate the malt
That lay in the house that Jack built.

This is the cock that crowed in the morn,
That waked the priest all shaven and shorn,
That married the man all tattered and torn,
That kissed the maiden all forlorn,
That milked the cow with the crumpled horn,
That tossed the dog,
That worried the cat,
That killed the rat,
That ate the malt
That lay in the house that Jack built.

This is the farmer sowing his corn,
That kept the cock that crowed in the morn,
That waked the priest all shaven and shorn,
That married the man all tattered and torn,
That kissed the maiden all forlorn,
That milked the cow with the crumpled horn,
That tossed the dog,
That worried the cat,
That killed the rat,
That ate the malt
That lay in the house that Jack built.

Anonymous

The Pobble who has no toes

The Pobble who has no toes
Had once as many as we;
When they said, 'Some day you may lose them all',
He replied, 'Fish fiddle de-dee!'
And his Aunt Jobiska made him drink,
Lavender water tinged with pink,
For she said, 'The world in general knows
There's nothing so good for a Pobble's toes!'

The Pobble who has no toes,
Swam across the Bristol Channel;
But before he set out he wrapped his nose
In a piece of scarlet flannel.
For his Aunt Jobiska said, 'No harm
Can come to his toes if his nose is warm,
And its perfectly known that a Pobble's toes
Are safe – provided he minds his nose.'

The Pobble swam fast and well,
And when boats and ships came near him
He tinkledy-binkledy-winkled a bell,
So that all the world could hear him.
And all the Sailors and Admirals cried,
When they saw him nearing the further side,
'He has gone to fish, for his Aunt Jobiska's
Runcible Cat with the crimson whiskers!'

But before he touched the shore,
The shore of the Bristol Channel,
A sea-green porpoise carried away
His wrapper of scarlet flannel.
And when he came to observe his feet
Formerly garnished with toes so neat,
His face at once became forlorn
On perceiving that all his toes were gone!

And nobody ever knew
From that dark day to the present,
Whoso had taken the Pobble's toes,
In a manner so far from pleasant.
Whether the shrimps or crawfish grey,
Or crafty Mermaids stole them away,
Nobody knew; and nobody knows
How the Pobble was robbed of his twice five toes!

The Pobble who has no toes
Was placed in a friendly Bark,
And they rowed him back, and carried him up,
To his Aunt Jobiska's Park.
And she made him a feast at his earnest wish
Of eggs and buttercups fried with fish,
And she said – 'It's a fact that the whole world knows,
That Pobbles are happier without their toes!'

Edward Lear

The Rock-a-By Lady

The Rock-a-By Lady from Hushaby Street
Comes stealing, comes creeping.
The poppies they hang from her head to her feet,
And each hath a dream that is tiny and fleet.
She bringeth her poppies to you, my sweet,
When she findeth you sleeping!

There is one little dream of a beautiful drum,
'Rub-a-dub!' it goeth.
There is one little dream of a big sugar-plum,
And lo! Thick and fast the other dreams come,
Of popguns that bang, and tin tops that hum,
And a trumpet that bloweth!

And dollies peep out of those wee little dreams
With laughter and singing.
And boats go a-floating on silvery streams,
And the stars peek-a-boo with their own misty gleams,
And up, up and up, where Mother Moon beams,
The fairies go winging!

Would you dream all these dreams that are tiny and fleet?
They'll come to you sleeping.
So shut the two eyes that are weary, my sweet,
For the Rock-a-By Lady from Hushaby Street
With poppies that hang from her head to her feet,
Comes stealing, comes creeping.

Eugene Field

Jack Frost

The door was shut, as doors should be,
Before you went to bed last night;
But Jack Frost has got in, you see,
And left your window silver white.

He must have waited till you slept;
And not a single word he spoke,
But pencilled o'er the panes and crept
Away again before you woke.

And now you cannot see the hills
Nor fields that stretch beyond the lane;
But there are fairer things than these
His fingers traced on every pane.

Rocks and castles towering high;
Hills and dales and streams and fields;
And knights in armour riding by,
With nodding plumes and shining shields.

And here are little boats, and there
Big ships with sails spread to the breeze;
And yonder, palm trees waving fair
Or islands set in silver seas.

And butterflies with gauzy wings;
And herds of cows and flocks of sheep;
And fruit and flowers and all the things
You see when you are sound asleep.

For creeping softly underneath
The door, when all the lights are out,
Jack Frost takes every breath you breathe
And knows the things you think about.

He paints them on the window pane,
In fairy lines with frozen steam;
And when you wake you see again
The lovely things you saw in dream.

Gabriel Setoun

Acknowledgements

We wish to thank the following for permission to use copyright poems:

WALTER DE LA MARE: Silver, Someone and The Fly by permission of The Literary Trustees of Walter de la Mare and the Society of Authors as their representative. ELEANOR FARJEON: The Night Will Never Stay, A Kitten and Cat! from Silver, Sand and Snow, published by Michael Joseph by permission of David Higham Associates Ltd. ROSE FYLEMAN: The Balloon Man, Fairies and A Fairy Went A-Marketing from Fairies and Chimneys by permission of the society of Authors as the literary representative of the estate of Rose Fyleman. PERCY H ILOTT: The Witch from Songs of English Childhood by permission of J.M.Dent and Sons Ltd. JAMES KIRKUP: The Lonely Scarecrow from Refusal to Conform by permission of Mr James Kirkup and Oxford University Press. ROGER MCGOUGH: Mrs Moon from Sky in the Pie reprinted by permission of A.D. Peters and Co Ltd. SPIKE MILLIGAN: On the Ning Nang Nong by permission of Spike Milligan Productions Ltd. OGDEN NASH: The Duck from Verses from 1929 On © 1936 by the Curtis Publishing Company, first appeared in the Saturday Evening Post, by permission of Andre Deutsch Ltd and Little Brown and Co, Boston, USA. JACK PRELUTSKY: The Hippopotamus from Zoo Doings © 1970, 1983 by Jack Prelutsky by permission of Greenwillow Books (A Division of William Morrow and Company). JAMES REEVES: If Pigs Could Fly from James Reeves – The Complete Poems by permission of Laura Cecil for and on behalf of James Reeves' Estate. Reprinted by permission of James Reeves' Estate. THEODORE ROETHKE: The Serpent © 1950 from the book, The Collected Poems of Theodore Roethke reprinted by permission of Doubleday and Co Inc, and Faber and Faber Ltd. CLIVE SANSOM: The Witches' Call from The Golden Unicorn published by Methuen Books Ltd by Permission of David Higham Associates Ltd. IAN SERRAILLIER: The Little Wee Man from I'll Tell You a Tale © 1973 - 1976. GABRIEL SETOUN: Jack Frost by permission of The Bodley Head Ltd from The Child World by Gabriel Setoun. OSBERT SITWELL: Winter the Huntsman from Selected Poems by permission of Duckworth and Co Ltd and David Higham Associates. MAJORIE WILSON: The Little Things That Happen by permission of Basil Blackwell. RAYMOND WILSON: The Traveller from Times Delight © Raymond Wilson.